A Special Gift

for:

from:

date:

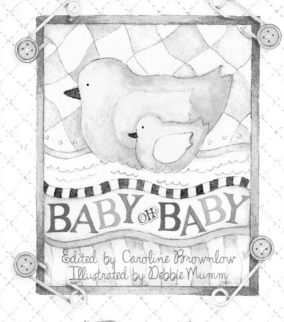

BABY OH BABY

Edited by Caroline Brownlow
Illustrated by Debbie Mumm

Little Treasures
Miniature Books

Friend
Grandmother
Grandmothers Are for Loving
Happiness Is Homemade
Mom, I Love You
My Sister, My Friend
Quiet Moments of Inspiration
Seasons of Friendship
Sister
Tea Time Friends
They Call It Golf

Dear Mom and Dad,

It's awfully hard right now you see,
To tell you what I'm thinking.
I'm getting bigger day by day,
I'm not here just a dreaming.
So when you hear my coos and whispers,
You'll know they have a meaning.
They mean, "I love you very much,"
And when is my next feeding?

A NOTE FROM BABY

Our children are living messages
we send to a time and place we
will not see.

ANONYMOUS

A baby is God's opinion that
the world should go on.

CARL SANDBURG

Children are a gift from the Lord.

PSALM 127:3

Nothing creates a firmer belief in heredity than having a beautiful baby.

ANONYMOUS

Babies are such a nice way
to start people.

DON HEROLD

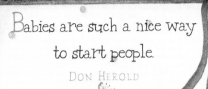

From the lips of
children and infants you
have ordained praise.

PSALM 8:2

Nothing you do for children
is ever wasted.

GARRISON KEILLOR

There are 152 distinctly different ways of holding a baby ~ and all are right.

HEYWOOD BROUN

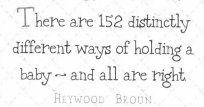

Children are a bridge to heaven.

ANCIENT PROVERB

All things bright
and beautiful,
All creatures great
and small,
All things wise
and wonderful,
The Lord God made them all.

CECIL F. ALEXANDER

A babe in house is a
well-spring of pleasure,
a messenger of peace
and love, a resting
place for innocence on
earth, a link between
angels and men.

MARTIN F. TUPPER

The best thing to spend on your
child is your time.

ANONYMOUS

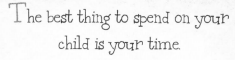

A babe is nothing but a bundle
of possibilities

HENRY WARD BEECHER

Give a little love to a child,
and you get a great deal back.

JOHN RUSKIN

I love these little people;
and it is not a slight
thing, when they, who
are so fresh from
God, love us.

CHARLES DICKENS

The Whole Duty
of Children

A child should always say what's true
And speak when he is spoken to;
And behave mannerly at table,
At least as far as he is able.

ROBERT LOUIS STEVENSON

Thank Heaven for Little Girls

Little girl to mother: "If Daddy can't get all his work finished at the office, why don't they put him in a slower group?"

ANONYMOUS

A happy childhood is one
of the best gifts that
parents have in their power
to bestow.

R. CHOLMONDELEY

A rich man is one who when
his pockets are empty,
his children fill his arms.

And whoever welcomes a little child like this in My name welcomes Me.

MATTHEW 18:5

RUBBER · DUCKY ·

Baby Dear

Where did you come from, baby dear?
Out of the everywhere into here.
Where did you get those eyes of blue?
Out of the sky as I came through.
What makes your cheek like a warm white rose?
I saw something better than anyone knows.

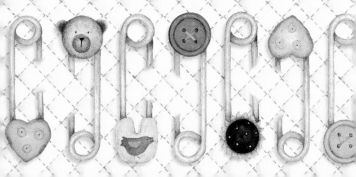

Where did you get this pearly ear?
God spoke, and it came out to hear.
Feet, whence did you come, you darling things?
From the same box as the cherubs' wings.
How did they all just come to be you?
God thought about me, and so I grew.
But how did you come to us, you dear?
God thought about you, and so I am here.

GEORGE MACDONALD

A child reaches for your hand
and touches your heart.

ANONYMOUS

A child does not need to be
parented. He needs to be
mothered and fathered.

ZAN THOMPSON

FEATHERED NEST

· ROCK · a · bye · Babies ·

munch! munch! munch! munch!

Thank Heaven for Little Boys

A boy can learn a lot from
a dog: obedience, loyalty, and
the importance of turning around
three times before lying down.

ROBERT BENCHLEY

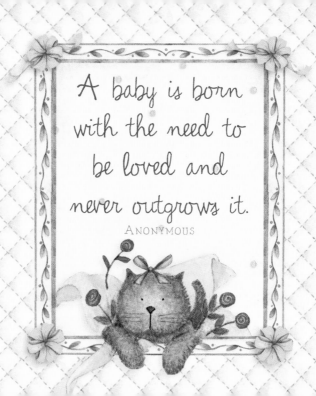

A baby is born with the need to be loved and never outgrows it.

ANONYMOUS

Homes are the building blocks of civilization.
ARNOLD TOYNBEE

A child brings hope with it and forward looking thoughts.
PROVERB

You are bone of my bones, and flesh of my flesh.
GENESIS 2:23

Roots and Wings

There are only two lasting
bequests we can hope to give
our children. One of these
is roots, the other wings.

HODDING CARTER

Just Like Sponges

Babies are like sponges.
They absorb all your strength and
leave you limp. But give them a
squeeze and you get it all back.

ANONYMOUS

Every baby comes with the message that God is not yet discouraged.

RABINDRANATH TAGORE

A Hundred Years From Now...

it will not matter what my bank
account was, the sort of house
I lived in, or the kind of car I
drove. But the world will be very
different because I was important
in the life of my child.

ANONYMOUS

No one who has ever brought up
a child can doubt for a moment
that love is literally the life-giving
fluid of human existence.

DR. SMILEY BLANTON

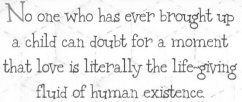

More babies are spoiled because
the mother won't spank Grandma.

ANONYMOUS

Children are the hands by which
we take hold of heaven.

HENRY WARD BEECHER

A baby enters your home and makes so much noise for twenty years you can hardly stand it—then departs, leaving the house so silent you think you'll go mad.

DR. J.A. HOLMES

Children are true connoisseurs. What's precious to them has no price—only value.

BEL KAUFMAN

A Grandparents Love

The importance of grandparents in the life of little children is im~measurable. A young child with the good fortune to have grandparents near by benefits in countless ways. It has a place to share its joys, its sorrows, to find a sympathetic and patient listener, to be loved.

EDWARD WAKIN

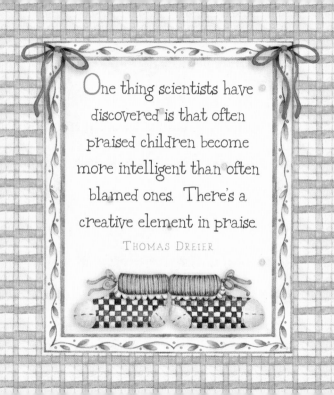

One thing scientists have discovered is that often praised children become more intelligent than often blamed ones. There's a creative element in praise.

THOMAS DREIER

A small child who was
getting upset and ready to
throw a fit was told,
"You can just be happy in the
same pants you're mad in."

HOLLY DAVIDSON

You dear children,
are from God.

1 JOHN 4:4

A baby in your lap may dampen your spirits.

ANONYMOUS

Every baby
needs a lap.

B. Weinninger
and
H. Rabin

As for me and my house,
we will serve the Lord.

JOSHUA 24:15

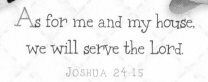

A baby—the most powerful
of powerless creatures.

ANONYMOUS

There's nothing
like a family.

AMERICAN PROVERB

Children Are

Children are God's apostles,
sent forth, day by day, to preach
of love, and hope and peace.

Children are likely
to live up to what
you believe of them.

LADY BIRD JOHNSON

Children
need love, especially
when they do
not deserve it.

HAROLD S. HULBERT